MW00635297

A Family Easter Celebration

Art Credits

Page IV: *I Am* © Simon Dewey. Courtesy of Altus Fine Art. For print information, go to www.altusfineart.com.

Page 2: *Triumphal Entry* © Liz Lemon Swindle. Used with permission from Foundation Arts. For print information, go to www.foundationarts.com or call 1-800-366-2781.

Page 5: *The Last Supper* by Carl Heinrich Bloch, courtesy of Det Nationalhistoriske Museum på Frederiksborg, Hillerød.

Page 6: *Last Supper* © Liz Lemon Swindle. Used with permission from Foundation Arts. For print information, go to www.foundationarts.com or call 1-800-366-2781.

Page 9: *In Humility* © Simon Dewey. Courtesy of Altus Fine Art. For print information, go to www.altusfineart.com.

Page 10: *Pure in Heart* © Simon Dewey. Courtesy of Altus Fine Art. For print information, go to www.altusfineart.com.

Page 13: *O My Father* © Simon Dewey. Courtesy of Altus Fine Art. For print information, go to www.altusfineart.com.

Page 18: *Behold the Man* © Simon Dewey. Courtesy of Altus Fine Art. For print information, go to www.altusfineart.com.

Page 21: *Gray Day* © J. Kirk Richards. For more information, visit www.jkirkrichards.com

Page 22–23: *He Is Not Here* © Walter Rane, 2004. For more information, visit www.walterrane.com.

Page 24–25: *Hope* © Liz Lemon Swindle. Used with permission from Foundation Arts. For print information, go to www.foundationarts.com or call 1-800-366-2781.

Page 27: *Why Weepest Thou?* © Liz Lemon Swindle. Used with permission from Foundation Arts. For print information, go to www.foundationarts.com or call 1-800-366-2781.

Page 28: *The Road to Emmaus* © Liz Lemon Swindle. Used with permission from Foundation Arts. For print information, go to www.foundationarts.com or call 1-800-366-2781.

Page 31: *The Ascension of Jesus* by Harry Anderson © Intellectual Reserve, Inc.

Page 35: *Grace and Truth* © Simon Dewey. Courtesy of Altus Fine Art. For print information, go to www.altusfineart.com.

Text by Kate Robinson Reschke
Front Cover: *He Lives* © Simon Dewey. Courtesy of Altus Fine Art. For print information, go to www.altusfineart.com.
Cover design copyright © 2017 Covenant Communications, Inc.
Published by Covenant Communications, Inc.
American Fork, Utah

Copyright © 2017 Covenant Communications, Inc.
All rights reserved. No part of this book may be reproduced in any format or in any medium without the written permission of the publisher, Covenant Communications, Inc., P. O. Box 416, American Fork, UT 84003. The views expressed within this work are the sole responsibility of the author and do not necessarily reflect the position of Covenant Communications, Inc., or any other entity.

Printed in China
First Printing: March 2017

22 21 20 19 18 17   10 9 8 7 6 5 4 3 2 1

ISBN: 978-1-68047-043-7

A Family Easter Celebration

Rejoicing in the Triumph of Christ through Scripture and Song

The noted poet Percy Bysshe Shelley once asked, "If winter comes, can spring be far behind?" Spring is beautiful precisely because it signifies the conclusion of the dark and cold of winter. New life approaches. Life-giving water abounds. Buds begin to appear on the trees, long since bereft of their leaves by the harsh realities of winter. Winter melting into spring is a beautiful reminder of what Lehi taught: "For it must needs be, that there is an opposition in all things. If not so . . . righteousness could not be brought to pass, neither wickedness, neither holiness nor misery, neither good nor bad" (2 Nephi 2:11).

Surely the Savior understood this, even in His perfect life. Before the glory of His Resurrection, He had to bear the horrors of Gethsemane and the cross. Before He completed His Atonement, His rescue, of all mankind, He suffered incomprehensible agony. Before the spring of His Resurrection, He endured the winter of suffering. How appropriate then that we have come to celebrate the most magnificent event in human history during the season symbolic of new life.

Easter gives us the opportunity to remember and give thanks for our Savior. Because of Him, we can be exalted. May this book help you and your family fill your home with the Spirit as you worship and praise Him this Easter season.

"He is not here: for he is risen."

—MATTHEW 28:6

He Is Risen!

With dignity ♩ = 92–104

1. He is ris - en! He is ris - en! Tell it out with
2. Come with high and ho - ly hymn - ing; Chant our Lord's tri -
3. He is ris - en! He is ris - en! He hath o - pened

joy - ful voice. He has burst his three days' pris - on;
um - phant lay. Not one dark - some cloud is dim - ming
heav - en's gate. We are free from sin's dark pris - on,

Let the whole wide earth re - joice. Death is con - quered,
Yon - der glo - rious morn - ing ray, Break - ing o'er the
Ris - en to a ho - lier state. And a bright - er

man is free. Christ has won the vic - to - ry.
pur - ple east, Sym - bol of our Eas - ter feast.
Eas - ter beam On our long - ing eyes shall stream.

Words: Cecil Frances Alexander, 1818–1895
Music: Joachim Neander, 1650–1680

Mark 16:6–7
Mosiah 16:7–9

Following the deliverance of the children of Israel from Egyptian captivity, the Lord instructed the people of Moses to remember His mercy in delivering them from bondage. In response, the Israelites instituted the Passover to commemorate the night they were spared from the destroying angel that brought death upon the firstborn in the land of Egypt. An important part of the eight-day celebration is the Passover Feast. It was in anticipation of this special meal that Jesus and His disciples made their way to Jerusalem, where Peter and John had secured a location for their Passover supper.

From high atop the Mount of Olives, Jesus looked down on Jerusalem. It had long been foretold that the Messiah would ride into the Holy City on the back of a young donkey, and the moment had come for the prophecy to be fulfilled that said, "Rejoice greatly, O daughter of Zion; shout, O daughter of Jerusalem: behold, thy King cometh unto thee: he is just, and having salvation; lowly, and riding upon an ass, and upon a colt the foal of an ass" (Zechariah 9:9). Jesus approached two of His disciples and made a special request: He asked that they descend into the city, where they would find a donkey and a colt tied in a doorway. The Savior instructed them to untie the animals and bring them back up the mountain to Him (Mark 11:2). He further advised, "If any man say ought unto you, ye shall say, The Lord hath need of them; and straightway he will send them" (Matthew 21:3).

The disciples faithfully did as Jesus asked, and made their way down the steep mountain slope. Soon they came upon the animals, just as Jesus had described. They received permission from the owner and climbed back up the mountainside with the donkeys. When they arrived at the place where Jesus waited, several of the disciples removed their coats and gently laid them over the colt's back to make a comfortable and clean place for the Savior to sit (see Mark 11:7; John 12:14–15).

And so the Savior rode down the Mount of Olives into Jerusalem on the back of the humble animal. His faithful followers within the city saw the approach and ran toward Jesus. They walked with Him along the road, removing their coats and laying them across the road for the donkey to walk on. Those who did not have coats spread palm tree branches on the ground before him (see Matthew 21:8). As they walked beside the Savior, the crowd of people joyfully shouted, "Hosanna to the Son of David: Blessed is he that cometh in the name of the Lord; Hosanna in the highest" (Matthew 21:9). Christ's followers recognized the fulfillment of the prophecy and knew that He was the promised Messiah.

*E*arly on the evening of the Passover feast, Jesus sat with His disciples at what was to be His last supper. To this small gathering, He said, "With desire I have desired to eat this passover with you before I suffer" (Luke 22:15). While the group of friends sat, Jesus took a portion of bread from the table. "And as they were eating, Jesus took bread, and blessed it, and brake it, and gave it to the disciples, and said, Take, eat; this is my body" (Matthew 26:26).

Next, He poured a glass of wine. "And he took the cup, and gave thanks, and gave it to them, saying, Drink ye all of it; For this is my blood of the new testament, which is shed for many for the remission of sins" (Matthew 26:27–28).

Jesus, the Very Thought of Thee

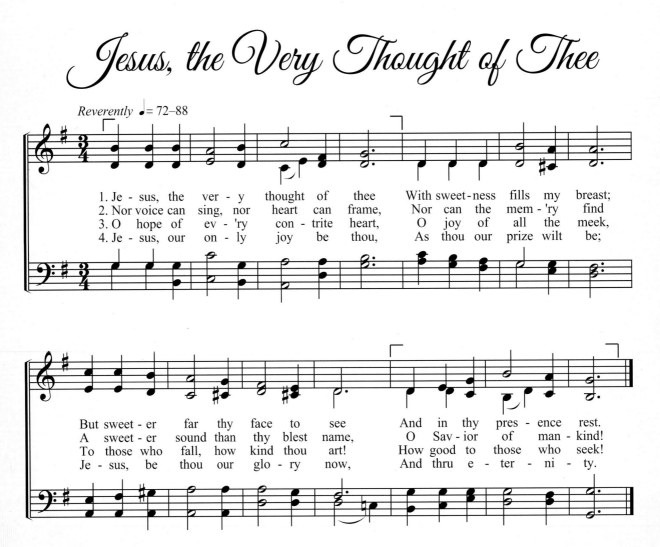

Reverently ♩ = 72–88

1. Je - sus, the ver - y thought of thee   With sweet - ness fills my breast;
2. Nor voice can sing, nor heart can frame,   Nor can the mem - 'ry find
3. O hope of ev - 'ry con - trite heart,   O joy of all the meek,
4. Je - sus, our on - ly joy be thou,   As thou our prize wilt be;

But sweet - er far thy face to see   And in thy pres - ence rest.
A sweet - er sound than thy blest name,   O Sav - ior of man - kind!
To those who fall, how kind thou art!   How good to those who seek!
Je - sus, be thou our glo - ry now,   And thru e - ter - ni - ty.

Text: Attr. to Bernard of Clairvaux, ca. 1091–1153; trans. by Edward Caswall, 1814–1878
Music: John B. Dykes, 1823–1876

Psalm 104:34
Enos 1:27

Lemon Swindle ©

To Think About Jesus

Words: Mabel Jones Gabbot, b. 1910. © 1969 LDS
Music: Robert Cundick, b. 1926. © 1969 LDS

Doctrine and Covenants 19:23–24

Come Follow Me

Humbly ♩ = 69–76

1. "Come, fol - low me," the Sav - ior said. Then let us
2. "Come, fol - low me," a sim - ple phrase, Yet truth's sub -
3. Is it e - nough a - lone to know That we must
4. Not on - ly shall we em - u - late His course while

in his foot - steps tread, For thus a - lone can
lime, ef - ful - gent rays Are in these sim - ple
fol - low him be - low, While trav - 'ling thru this
in this earth - ly state, But when we're freed from

we be one With God's own loved, be - got - ten Son.
words com - bined To urge, in - spire the hu - man mind.
vale of tears? No, this ex - tends to ho - lier spheres.
pres - ent cares, If with our Lord we would be heirs.

5. We must the onward path pursue
   As wider fields expand to view,
   And follow him unceasingly,
   Whate'er our lot or sphere may be.

6. For thrones, dominions, kingdoms, pow'rs,
   And glory great and bliss are ours,
   If we, throughout eternity,
   Obey his words, "Come, follow me."

Text: John Nicholson, 1839–1909
Music: Samuel McBurney, b. 1847

Matthew 4:19
2 Nephi 31:10–21

Simon Dewey

After Jesus and His disciples had finished their Passover supper, the Savior rose from the table and covered Himself with a towel as an apron. He then proceeded to kneel before each of His Apostles and, using a basin of water and His towel, wash their feet (see John 13:5). This supreme act of humility startled Simon Peter, who protested when Jesus came to him, saying, "Thou shalt never wash my feet" (John 13:8). The Savior used this experience as a teaching moment, telling Peter, "If I wash thee not, thou hast no part with me. . . . He that is washed needeth not save to wash his feet, but is clean every whit: and ye are clean, but not all" (John 13:8, 10).

In this statement, Jesus alludes to one man in particular—Judas Iscariot, who would betray the Lord. For thirty pieces of silver, Judas made a secret alliance with evil men, promising to deliver the Lord into their hands (see Matthew 26:15–16). This act of betrayal was unknown to the other Apostles, but Christ sorrowfully acknowledged the deception in a private conversation with Judas. Following their meal, the Lord released His betrayer into the night with the words, "That thou doest, do quickly" (John 13:27).

One of the most stirring pleas that Jesus made to His disciples concerned their treatment of their fellowman: "By this shall all men know that ye are my disciples, if ye have love one to another" (John 13:35). This invitation was designed to inspire all of His followers to convey the Christlike love that sets apart true disciples.

Love One Another

Reverently ♩ = 46–56

Duet
As I have loved you, Love one an - oth - er.

This new com - mand - ment: Love one an - oth - er.

By this shall men know Ye are my dis - ci - ples,

If ye have love One to an - oth - er.

Text and music: Luacine Clark Fox, b 1914, arr. © 1961 Luacine C. Fox.
Copyright renewed 1989. This hymn may be copied for incidental,
noncommercial church or home use.

John 13:34–35
1 John 4:11

*J*esus spent the final hours of His mortal ministry teaching His remaining eleven Apostles—preparing them to face the persecution that would come and instructing them on how to lead the Church in His absence. He spoke the words that His disciples dreaded, foretelling His death and Resurrection, as He said, "A little while, and ye shall not see me: and again, a little while, and ye shall see me, because I go to the Father" (John 16:16). Knowing of their sorrow at what was to come, the Savior offered powerful words of peace, saying, "These things I have spoken unto you, that in me ye might have peace. In the world ye shall have tribulation: but be of good cheer; I have overcome the world" (John 16:33). And with great compassion, He had already promised them the Holy Ghost: "I will not leave you comfortless: I will come to you" (John 14:18).

At the conclusion of this final gathering of His disciples, He offered a powerful prayer. He presented His Father a final report of His earthly ministry, closing with the words, "I have glorified thee on the earth: I have finished the work which thou gavest me to do" (John 17:4). He also made a poignant appeal in behalf of his faithful disciples and all those who believe in Him: "I pray for them: I pray not for the world, but for them which thou hast given me; for they are thine. . . . Neither pray I for these alone, but for them also which shall believe on me through their word. . . . That the love wherewith thou hast loved me may be in them, and I in them" (John 17:9, 20, 26).

Following His closing prayer at the Passover feast, Jesus and His disciples left the darkened streets of the city, climbing the slope of the Mount of Olives to enter a small garden called Gethsemane. He left all His Apostles—except Peter, James, and John—at the entrance. As three men followed Jesus deeper into the grove, the Savior was overwhelmed with grief. "My soul is exceeding sorrowful, even unto death: tarry ye here, and watch with me" (Matthew 26:38). He knew that the burden He was to carry was His alone and asked those accompanying Him to wait and watch while He went on. Then, in the depths of the garden, He was overcome by the weight of His anguish and fell to the ground (see Matthew 26:39). The three Apostles heard His pleading words to the Father: "If it be possible, let this cup pass from me: nevertheless not as I will, but as thou wilt" (Matthew 26:39). However, physically exhausted, the disciples were soon unable to do as they were instructed.

Returning to the three men, Jesus was disappointed to find them sleeping. He asked sadly, "What, could ye not watch with me one hour?" (Matthew 26:40). He reminded them, "Watch and pray, that ye enter not into temptation: the spirit indeed is willing, but the flesh is weak" (Matthew 26:41). He then returned to His lonely task.

When Jesus returned once more to His disciples, He found that they had again succumbed to sleep. He retreated a third and final time, and pled for comfort, saying, "Father, if thou be willing, remove this cup from me: nevertheless not my will, but thine, be done. And there appeared an angel unto him from heaven, strengthening him. And being in an agony he prayed more earnestly: and his sweat was as it were great drops of blood falling down to the ground" (Luke 22:42–44). Even with a heavenly helper, Jesus's spiritual agony was so great that He bled from every pore (Mosiah 3:7). In that dark and lonely garden, Jesus Christ took upon Himself the sins of all mankind.

Gethsemane

Words & Music by Melanie Hoffman
Arranged by Roger Hoffman

1. Je - sus

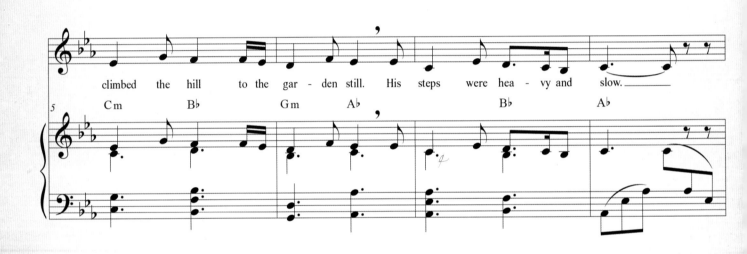

climbed the hill to the gar - den still. His steps were hea - vy and slow.

Love and a prayer took Him there to the place on-ly He could go.

Chorus

Geth - se - ma - ne. Je - sus loves me. So He went will - ing - ly ____ To Geth - se - ma - ne. 2. He felt all that was sad, wick - ed or bad, All the pain we would e - ver know While His friends were a - sleep He fought to keep His pro - mise made long a - go. ____

Bb   Eb   Bb   Eb   Ab
Bb   Ab   Bb   Cm
Cm   Bb   Gm7   Ab   Bb   Ab
Cm   Bb   Gm   Ab   Bb   Cm

As Jesus Christ suffered the sins of the world, Judas Iscariot was on his way to the garden with a group of Roman soldiers. His betrayal nearly complete, Judas led the group to place where Jesus waited with His disciples. Approaching the Savior, the traitor Judas kissed Christ on the cheek, to which the Lord responded, "Judas, betrayest thou the Son of man with a kiss?" (Luke 22:48).

Understanding what must happen, Jesus addressed the soldiers, asking, "Whom seek ye?" The guards replied, "Jesus of Nazareth," to which Jesus responded, "I am he" (John 18:4–5). Realizing the intent of the group that had approached them, the disciples attempted to fight off the crowd—even going so far as to injure one of the soldiers (see Matthew 26:51). With His characteristic selflessness and love, the Savior healed the soldier (see Luke 22:51) and calmed His disciples with a gentle reminder: "Thinkest thou that I cannot now pray to my Father, and he shall presently give me more than twelve legions of angels? But how then shall the scriptures be fulfilled, that thus it must be?" (Matthew 26:53–54). With these words, Christ was bound and led away to stand trial.

Christ was first taken to a meeting of Jewish leaders at the palace of Caiaphas, the high priest (see Matthew 26:57). The assembly sought any reason to put Jesus to death but were frustrated by their inability to find any witnesses or evidence of a crime. Finally, they asked Jesus one question: "I adjure thee by the living God," said Caiaphas, "that thou tell us whether thou be the Christ, the Son of God" (Matthew 26:63). Jesus answered, "I am: and ye shall see the Son of man sitting on the right hand of power, and coming in the clouds of heaven" (Mark 14:62). By claiming His divinity, Christ had given His accusers the offense they sought: the crime of blasphemy (see Mark 14:63–64).

The court of Jewish leaders proclaimed that this crime was worthy of death, a recommendation they made upon delivering Jesus into the hands of Pontius Pilate, the local government leader. Pilate was the only man with legal power to proclaim a sentence of death. The Jewish leaders presented their claim: "And they began to accuse him, saying, We found this fellow perverting the nation, and forbidding to give tribute to Caesar, saying that he himself is Christ a King" (Luke 23:2). Pilate asked Jesus, "Art thou the King of the Jews?" Jesus answered, "Thou sayest it" (Luke 23:3). However, upon learning that Jesus was Galilean, Pilate relinquished Christ to Herod, the leader who had jurisdiction over Galilee (Luke 23:6–7).

Herod was pleased when Jesus was brought before him. He had long heard tales of the Healer and hoped to see Him perform a mighty miracle (see Luke 23:8). Herod set about questioning the prisoner, but Christ remained silent. Herod and his men mocked the Savior, dressing Him in regal robes before finding no reason to condemn the prisoner to death. The decision was made to return Christ to Pilate for the final verdict of His fate.

Still believing Jesus innocent, Pilate presented Him before a gathering of priests, rulers, and citizens, and proclaimed, "I, having examined him before you, have found no fault in this man touching those things whereof ye accuse him: No, nor yet Herod: for I sent you to him; and, lo, nothing worthy of death is done unto him" (Luke 23:14–15).

A long-held tradition of the Passover celebration was the release of a single condemned prisoner. With his belief in Christ's innocence, Pilate asked the gathered crowd, "Whom will ye that I release unto you? Barabbas, or Jesus which is called Christ?" (Matthew 27:17). Given the choice between freeing Barrabas, a criminal and murderer, or Jesus Christ, the crowd made the fateful decision, electing to release Barrabas. Surprised, Pilate asked, "What shall I do then with Jesus which is called Christ?" to which the crowd responded, "Let him be crucified" (Matthew 27:22). The people had spoken, and "when Pilate saw that he could prevail nothing . . . he took water, and washed his hands before the multitude, saying, I am innocent of the blood of this just person: see ye to it. Then answered all the people, and said, His blood be on us, and on our children" (Matthew 27:24–25).

Following the verdict, the Savior was led into the palace by a company of royal guards. There, He was forced to put on a kingly robe and a sharp crown of twisted thorns (see Matthew 27:27–29). They did not believe He was a king, and the soldiers mocked and beat Him, shouting, "Hail, King of the Jews!" (John 19:3). The soldiers hoisted a heavy wooden cross onto Jesus's back and forced Him to begin the difficult walk across the city toward the hill called Golgotha (see John 19:17). Along the path, a Cyrenean man named Simon was called forward from the crowd to help the Savior carry His heavy burden (Matthew 27:32).

At the top of the hill, three crosses were raised. Jesus's hands and feet were cruelly nailed to the wooden boards, and He was lifted into the air to hang between two thieves. Jesus's only offense was written on a sign and attached to the cross: "Jesus of Nazareth The King of the Jews" (John 19:19). The cruelty of the crowd continued as the Savior hung in agony. They taunted, "Save thyself. If thou be the Son of God, come down from the cross. . . . He saved others; himself he cannot save. If he be the King of Israel, let him now come down from the cross, and we will believe him" (Matthew 27:40, 42). Jesus did not respond. He knew that through His sacrifice, He could save more than just His own life—He could save all mankind.

Text: Cecil Frances Alexander, 1818–1895
Music: John H. Gower, 1855–1922

John 19:16–20
Hebrews 13:12

$\mathcal{A}$s He hung on the cross, darkness slowly began to cover the land. Late in the afternoon, after many hours of suffering, Jesus Christ was overcome with anguish and cried, "My God, my God, why hast thou forsaken me?" (Matthew 27:46). The Savior felt alone, but He pressed on. Finally, late in the afternoon, Jesus took His final breath, uttering the words, "It is finished" (John 19:30). "Father, into thy hands I commend my spirit" (Luke 23:46). As His spirit left His body, the sun was dimmed, and a deep darkness covered the land (see Luke 23:44–45). It seemed that the day turned suddenly into night, and the entire earth shook (see Matthew 27:51). After the turmoil ceased, one Roman soldier exclaimed, "Truly this man was the Son of God" (Mark 15:39).

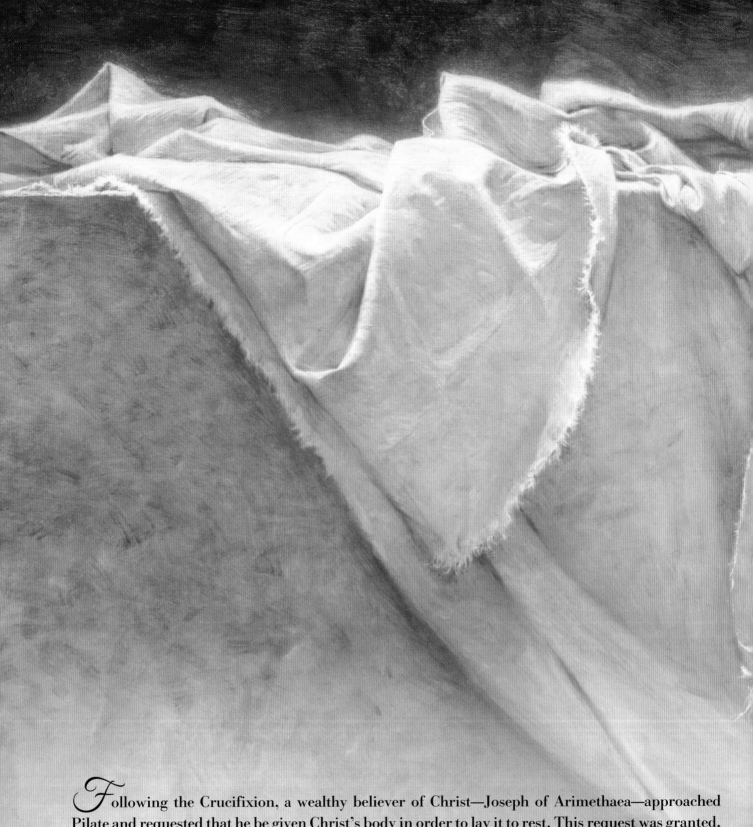

$\mathcal{F}$ollowing the Crucifixion, a wealthy believer of Christ—Joseph of Arimethaea—approached Pilate and requested that he be given Christ's body in order to lay it to rest. This request was granted, and Joseph took the Savior's body to his own tomb, where he reverently wrapped Jesus in clean linen, laid the body within, and rolled a massive stone to seal the entrance (see Matthew 27:57–60).

It was early morning, two days after the Savior's death; Mary Magdalene and two of her friends made their way to the tomb where Jesus's body had been placed (see Mark 16:1). When they arrived, their arms full of spices and perfume for His body, they were astonished to find that the stone blocking

the entrance to the tomb had been rolled away. Even more shocking was the sight of an angel of the Lord (see Mark 16:5).

The women were afraid, but the angel reassured them: "Fear not ye: for I know that ye seek Jesus, which was crucified. He is not here: for he is risen, as he said. Come, see the place where the Lord lay" (Matthew 28:5–6). When the women entered the dark tomb, they found that the angel had spoken the truth—the room was empty. The angel commanded them to go quickly and tell the disciples all that they had seen and heard. The women ran from the tomb to share the wonderful news (see Matthew 28:7–8).

When the disciples heard the women's account, they were shocked. Most dismissed the account as "idle tales" (Luke 24: 11), but Peter and John quickly made their way to the tomb to see for themselves (John 20:3). Finding it empty of all but the cloths that had been wrapped around Jesus, the disciples left the tomb, marveling over what could have happened.

Christ the Lord Is Risen Today

With exultation ♩ = 96–108

1. Christ the Lord is ris'n to - day,
2. Love's re - deem - ing work is done,
3. Lives a - gain our glo - rious King,

Al - le - lu - ia!

Sons of men and an - gels say,
Fought the fight, the vic - t'ry won,
Where, O death, is now thy sting?

Al - le - lu - ia!

Raise your joys and tri - umphs high,
Je - sus' ag - o - ny is o'er,
Once he died our souls to save,

Al - le - lu - ia!

Sing, ye heav'ns, and earth re - ply,
Dark - ness veils the earth no more,
Where thy vic - to - ry, O grave?

Al - le - lu - ia!

Text: Charles Wesley, 1707–1788
Music: Anon., *Lyra Davidica*, 1708

Matthew 28:5–6
1 Corinthians 15:20, 53–57

$\mathcal{A}$fter the others had left the empty tomb, Mary Magdalene remained, overcome with confusion. As tears filled her eyes, she perceived two heavenly messengers who asked her, "Woman, why weepest thou?"(John 20:13). She answered, expressing her concern about the location of Jesus's body. With that, a voice repeated the question, causing her to turn. "Woman, why weepest thou?" Supposing Him to be a gardener, Mary begged Him to tell her where the Lord had been hidden (see John 20:15). The stranger then spoke one word, "Mary." And all at once she knew Him. Mary exclaimed "Rabboni," or Master. Jesus instructed her not to touch Him, as He had not yet ascended to His Father, and tasked her with bearing witness to His disciples that Christ the Lord was truly risen.

$\mathcal{A}$ few days after the Crucifixion, two of Jesus's disciples were walking along the road from Jerusalem to the village of Emmaus. As they discussed all that had happened to their beloved Savior, they were joined by a third man. He walked by their side, asking "What manner of communications are these that ye have one to another, as ye walk, and are sad?" (Luke 24:17). The disciples told the man of Jesus's crucifixion and the women's discovery of His empty tomb: "And when they found not his body, they came, saying, that they had also seen a vision of angels, which said that he was alive" (Luke 24:23). When the group reached Emmaus that evening, the men kindly asked the stranger to join them for a meal (see Luke 24:29).

As the trio sat together, the stranger took the bread from the table, broke it, and blessed it. In that instant, the two disciples realized that the man was, in fact, Jesus Christ. At the very moment they recognized the Savior, He disappeared from sight. Overcome with emotion, the disciples returned to Jerusalem to testify to the other followers of Christ, "Saying, The Lord is risen indeed" (Luke 24:34).

How Great the Wisdom and the Love

Calmly ♩ = 66–76

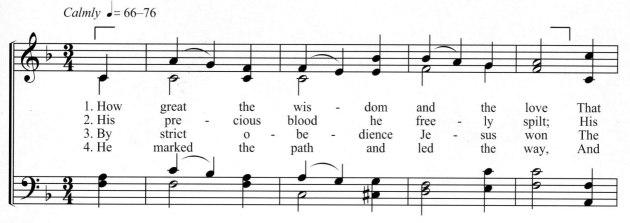

1. How great the wis - dom and the love That
2. His pre - cious blood he free - ly spilt; His
3. By strict o - be - dience Je - sus won The
4. He marked the path and led the way, And

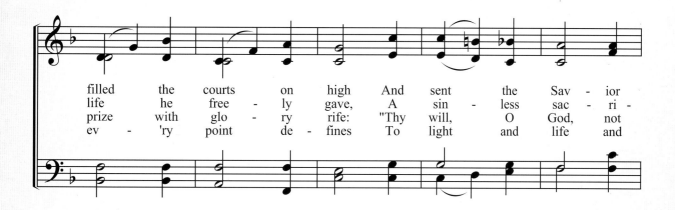

filled the courts on high And sent the Sav - ior
life he free - ly gave, A sin - less sac - ri -
prize with glo - ry rife: "Thy will, O God, not
ev - 'ry point de - fines To light and life and

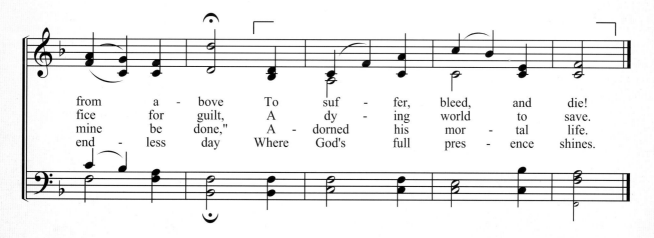

from a - bove To suf - fer, bleed, and die!
fice for guilt, A dy - ing world to save.
mine be done," A - dorned his mor - tal life.
end - less day Where God's full pres - ence shines.

5. In mem'ry of the broken flesh
   We eat the broken bread
   And witness with the cup, afresh,
   Our faith in Christ, our Head.

6. How great, how glorious, how complete,
   Redemption's grand design,
   Where justice, love, and mercy meet
   In harmony divine!

Text: Eliza R. Snow, 1804–1887
Music: Thomas McIntyre, 1833–1914
Verses 1, 2, 5, and 6 are especially appropriate for the sacrament.

Moses 4:1–2
Alma 42:14–15

Lord, I Would Follow Thee

Gently ♩ = 78–96

1. Sav - ior, may I learn to love thee, Walk the path that thou hast shown,
2. Who am I to judge an - oth - er When I walk im - per - fect - ly?
3. I would be my broth-er's keep-er; I would learn the heal-er's art.
4. Sav - ior, may I love my broth - er As I know thou lov - est me,

Pause to help and lift an - oth - er, Find - ing strength be - yond my own.
In the qui - et heart is hid - den Sor - row that the eye can't see.
To the wound - ed and the wea - ry I would show a gen - tle heart.
Find in thee my strength, my bea - con, For thy ser - vant I would be.

Sav - ior, may I learn to love thee — Lord, I would fol - low thee.
Who am I to judge an - oth - er? Lord, I would fol - low thee.
I would be my broth - er's keep - er — Lord, I would fol - low thee.
Sav - ior, may I love my broth - er — Lord, I would fol - low thee.

Text: Susan Evans McCloud, b. 1945. © 1985 LDS
Music: K. Newell Dayley, b. 1939. © 1985 LDS

John 13:34–35
1 John 3:16–19; 4:21

For forty days, the risen Christ walked among His disciples, continuing to teach them and prepare them for the responsibility of preaching the message of the gospel to all the world (see Acts 1:3). At the end of that period, the Savior led His disciples into a mountain (see Matthew 28:16).

Before ascending into His Father's presence, Christ gave His followers a charge: "Go ye therefore, and teach all nations, baptizing them in the name of the Father, and of the Son, and of the Holy Ghost: Teaching them to observe all things whatsoever I have commanded you: and, lo, I am with you alway, even unto the end of the world. Amen" (Matthew 28:19–20). With those final words, Jesus ascended into the sky. Surrounded by a magnificent cloud, the Savior of the world was lost from sight, His earthly mission fulfilled (see Acts 1:9).

"I am the resurrection, and the life: he that believeth in me, though he were dead, yet shall he live: And whosoever liveth and believeth in me shall never die" (John 11:25–26).

He Sent His Son

Words: Mabel Jones Gabbott, b. 1910
Music: Michael Finlinson Moody, b. 1941

Moroni 7:48; 3 Nephi 27:21
John 3:16; 13:15

© 1982 by Mabel Jones Gabbott and Michael Finlinson Moody. Arr. © 1989 IRI.
This song may be copied for incidental, noncommercial church or home use.

33

I Know That my Redeemer Lives

Peacefully ♩ = 72–84

Unison

1. I know that my Re - deem - er lives. What com - fort this
2. He lives to grant me rich sup - ply. He lives to guide
3. He lives, my kind, wise heav'n - ly Friend. He lives and loves
4. He lives! All glo - ry to his name! He lives, my Sav -

sweet sen - tence gives! He lives, he lives, who once was
me with his eye. He lives to com - fort me when
me to the end. He lives, and while he lives, I'll
ior, still the same. Oh, sweet the joy this sen - tence

dead. He lives, my ev - er - liv - ing Head.
faint. He lives to hear my soul's com - plaint.
sing. He lives, my Proph - et, Priest, and King.
gives: "I know that my Re - deem - er lives!"

Harmony

He lives to bless me with his love. He lives to
He lives to si - lence all my fears. He lives to
He lives and grants me dai - ly breath. He lives, and
He lives! All glo - ry to his name! He lives, my

34

plead for me a - bove.
wipe a - way my tears.
I shall con - quer death.
Sav - ior, still the same.

He lives my hun - gry soul to
He lives to calm my trou - bled
He lives my man - sion to pre -
Oh, sweet the joy this sen - tence

feed. He lives to bless in time of need.
heart. He lives all bless - ings to im - part.
pare. He lives to bring me safe - ly there.
gives: "I know that my Re - deem - er lives!"

Text: Samuel Medley, 1738–1799. Included
  in the first LDS hymnbook, 1835.
Music: Lewis D. Edwards, 1858–1921

Job 19:25
Psalm 104:33–34

35

Points to Ponder

- Why were Jesus's followers in Jerusalem so happy to see His triumphal entry into the city?

- What sacred ordinance did Jesus introduce at the Last Supper?

- What promises did Jesus ask us to make when we take the sacrament?

- Why did Jesus wash His disciples' feet? How did they react?

- What was the reason for Jesus's suffering in the Garden of Gethsemane?

- How has the Atonement blessed you in your life?

- What would have happened to us all if no Atonement had been made?

- How does the knowledge that Jesus suffered for your sins make you feel? How does it influence your actions?

- How did Jesus treat those who arrested Him? What does this demonstrate about His character?

- Why didn't Jesus save Himself from crucifixion?

- Why was the tomb empty?

- How did Christ's followers react to the empty tomb?

- How did Jesus spend His time on Earth following His Resurrection?

- What were Jesus's final instructions to His disciples?